AMERICA'S MOST WINNING TEAMS™

KANSAS BASKETBALL

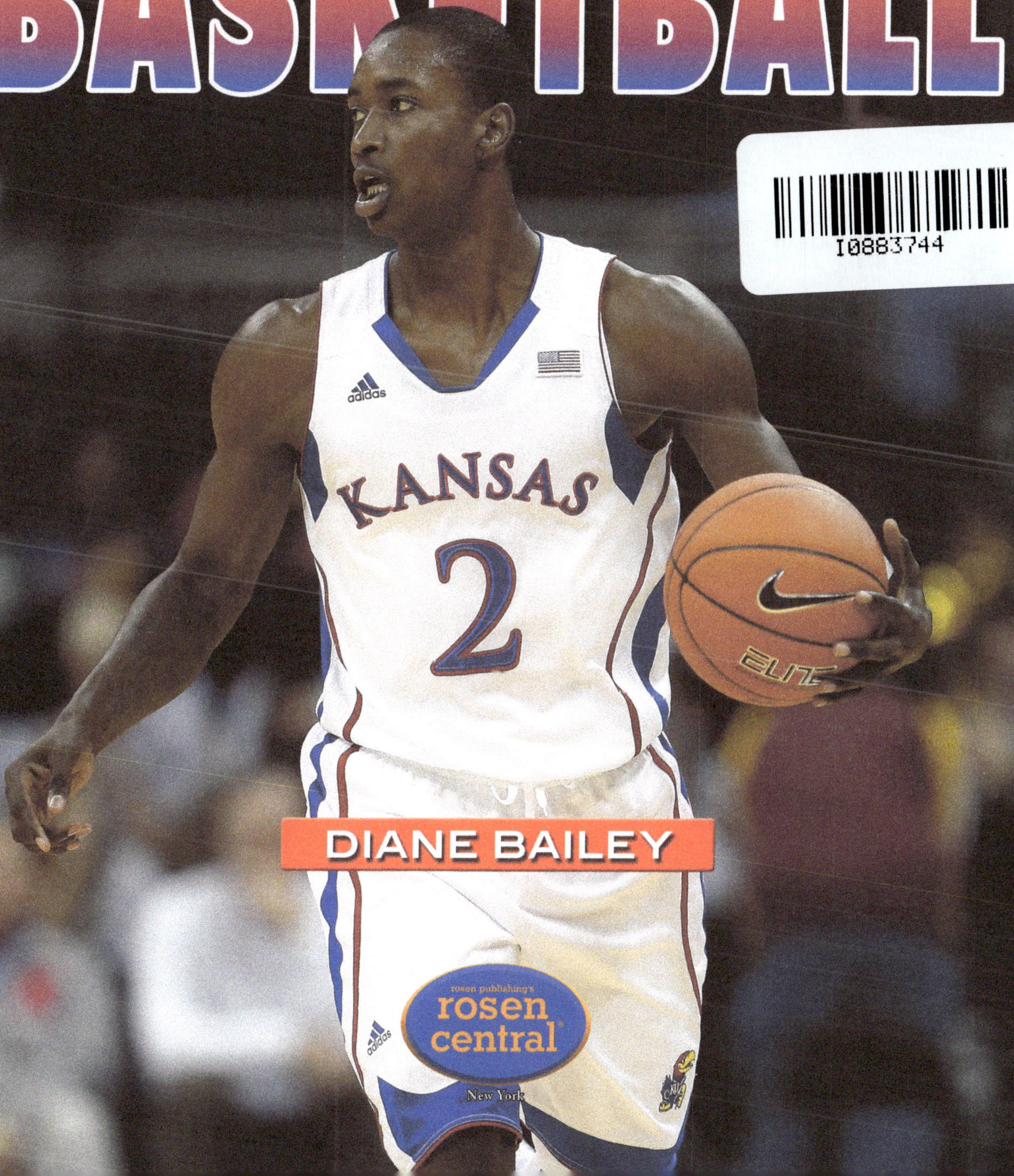

DIANE BAILEY

rosen publishing's
rosen central®
New York

Published in 2014 by The Rosen Publishing Group, Inc.
29 East 21st Street, New York, NY 10010

First Edition

Library of Congress Cataloging-in-Publication Data

Bailey, Diane, 1966-
Kansas basketball/Diane Bailey.—1st ed.—New York: Rosen, c2014
p. cm.—(America's most winning teams)
Includes bibliographical references and index.
ISBN: 978-1-4488-9405-5 (Library Binding)
ISBN: 978-1-4488-9429-1 (Paperback)
ISBN: 978-1-4488-9430-7 (6-pack)
1. Kansas Jayhawks (Basketball team)—History—Juvenile literature. 2. University of Kansas—Basketball—History—Juvenile literature. I. Title.
GV885.43.U52 .B35 2014
796.323'630978165

Manufactured in the United States of America

CPSIA Compliance Information: Batch #S13YA: For further information, contact Rosen Publishing, New York, New York, at 1-800-237-9932.

CONTENTS

INTRODUCTION

Pay Heed All Who Enter: Beware of the Phog.

This message is written on a banner that hangs in Allen Fieldhouse, where the Kansas University basketball team plays. The words sound like a warning, but any team who comes to play against the Jayhawks probably already knows what it's up against. Kansas is consistently one of the best teams in the country for basketball—and the fans won't let anyone forget it.

At home games, sixteen thousand people are crammed into the bleachers. A quarter of those are students, who stand up through the entire game. Most of them are dressed in the school colors, crimson and blue. They are not afraid to make some noise. After singing the school song, the crowd revs up into the traditional chant: "Rock, Chalk, Jayhawk." As the Kansas players are introduced, fans tear paper into confetti and shower it onto the floor. The Jayhawks haven't won yet—they haven't even started playing—but at Kansas, the devotion starts long before the game clock does.

In its history, Kansas has won three NCAA (National Collegiate Athletic Association) championships. It also has dozens of conference titles to its name—more than any other Division

A huge stylized Jayhawk decorates the court of Allen Fieldhouse, where fans fill the arena when the Kansas Jayhawks basketball team plays. Here, they face the Florida Atlantic Owls in 2011.

I team. (Division I is for the highest level of play.) The school also has the most winning seasons of any Division I team and ranks second in the total number of wins, with more than two thousand. Many players who have starred on the court for Kansas have gone on to have successful careers in the NBA (National Basketball Association). In 2008, the sports network ESPN ranked the program the second most prestigious in the country, behind only North Carolina's Duke University.

The basketball tradition at Kansas is 115 years strong, but its history is even longer. It stretches back to the origin of the sport itself. It all started with a cold winter and a shortage of boxes.

CHAPTER 1

THE TRADITION STARTS

In Massachusetts, physical education teacher James Naismith faced a challenge. He wanted to come up with a sport that students could play indoors during bad winter weather. His idea was a game in which players would pass a large ball between them. They would score points by throwing the ball into a box mounted over their heads. To try out his game, Naismith asked the school's custodian for some boxes. There weren't any. Instead, the man produced a couple of empty peach baskets. Basketball was born. It was immediately a hit in the Northeast, but it was soon to become even more popular.

BASKETBALL COMES TO KANSAS

In 1898, Naismith came to teach at the University of Kansas, where he started a basketball team. The team played its first game against a YMCA club from nearby Kansas City. The university men lost, 16–5, but the team improved quickly. In its first season, Kansas posted a record of seven wins and four losses.

Naismith coached at Kansas until 1907. The Kansas teams actually lost more games than they won during

Naismith's time. He is the only Kansas coach to have a losing record overall. However, Naismith's legacy at Kansas was bigger than the points on the scoreboard. He laid the groundwork for what would eventually become one of the most respected and successful basketball programs in the country.

Although his title was "coach," Naismith acted more like an official. As long as his players followed the rules (which he had invented), they could play however they wanted. In fact, he once famously said, "You can't coach basketball; you just play it."

James Naismith, a physical education teacher from Massachusetts, invented the game of basketball in the late 1800s and introduced it to the University of Kansas.

When Naismith said this, he was talking to a man named Forrest Allen. Allen doubted Naismith's statement. He had played for Naismith during the 1905–1906 season. After leaving Kansas for several years to get a medical degree, he returned in 1919. At that time, he began a thirty-five-year career as head coach of the Jayhawks. By the time he left, no one believed that basketball could not be coached.

THE DOCTOR IS IN

Forrest Allen did not dream of being a coach. When he came back to Kansas, he was hired as the athletics director. But

THE JAYHAWK MASCOT

The Jayhawk that is Kansas's mascot doesn't look like any real bird. That's because it isn't. The term "Jayhawk" is short for Jayhawkers. Jayhawkers lived in Kansas in the mid-1800s. They were people who opposed slavery and often battled pro-slavery forces in neighboring states such as Missouri. In 1912, Henry Maloy shortened the term to "Jayhawk" and came up with the idea of creating a bird image to represent the university. Later, another professor said that the bird was a cross between the noisy and argumentative blue jay and the skillful hunter, the sparrow hawk.

that plan lasted only a few months. After the basketball coach suddenly stepped down, Allen had no time to find someone else. He appointed himself the new coach.

With a voice that sounded like a foghorn, he acquired the nickname "Phog." His players, however, usually called him "Doc." Allen believed the most important part of coaching was keeping his team healthy. On game days, players followed a strict schedule. They rested, had a little light exercise, and then ate. Before the team took the court, Allen made the rounds in the locker room. He stopped before each player and asked, "Are you ready?" One time, a player said "no." The answer surprised Allen, who was used to hearing "yes." The player sat the game out.

The Kansas team began to come together during the early 1920s. In 1922 and again in 1923, the Jayhawks won the national championship sponsored by the Helms Foundation (before the days of the NCAA championship). Some of Kansas's early stars played during this time. All-American Charlie Black became the first KU player to score 1,000 points in his career. Another key player, Paul Endacott, starred in a game

His players were comfortable on the court, so that's where legendary coach Phog Allen held an informal meeting with members of the Jayhawks' 1940 team to review play formations.

against Missouri during the 1922–1923 season. On the day of the game, things didn't start well for the Jayhawks. The team vehicle broke down, and the players had to walk 3 miles (4.8 kilometers). At the game, however, Kansas rallied from a deficit. They took a small lead with two minutes remaining. That's when Endacott made an amazing effort. When the referee tossed the ball up—a jump ball—to determine which team got it, Endacott was there every time. He won sixteen jump balls in a row. That kept Kansas in the lead as the clock ran down.

Throughout the end of the 1920s and into the 1930s, Kansas consistently did well. In 1940, the team went to the NCAA finals. However, the team lost to Indiana. It would be ten more years before Kansas reached another NCAA final.

A GAME CHANGER

Phog Allen had some of his own ideas about how to play basketball. Some officials thought each player should get only one dribble each time he had the ball. Allen thought this would slow the game down too much. In 1927, he banded together with other coaches to protest the idea. The dribble was saved. Allen also helped put in a place a rule that gave the offensive team only ten seconds to bring the ball past half court. To prove this rule was necessary, in one game he had his players literally sit down on the court, while one held the ball idly. With no time limit, the clock ticked away. The next year, there was no sitting. Ten seconds was the new rule.

TWO CHAMPIONSHIPS

Allen had helped establish the NCAA tournament in 1939, but the Jayhawks had not won it. Allen decided to change that. In 1947, he set a goal for the Jayhawks to win the championship in five years, 1952.

The 1951–1952 season was good for the Jayhawks, who ended with a 22–2 record. The two losses had come right in a row, in the middle of the season. They set Doc Allen thinking. He called on his assistant coach, Dick Harp, for help. What should the Jayhawks do differently? Harp came up with a new defensive strategy that helped turn the team around. Just as Allen had planned, Kansas went on to the NCAA tournament.

Led by senior Clyde Lovellette, a powerful, 6'9" (2.06 meters) "big man," the Jayhawks plowed through their opening tournament games. They defeated Texas Christian, then St. Louis, and then Santa Clara. Finally, they faced St. John's in the finals. Kansas won handily, 80–63. Lovellette scored

Teammates jockey for position while the Jayhawks' big man, the 6'9" (2.06 m) center Clyde Lovellette, holds the ball up during a practice at New York's Madison Square Garden in 1950.

33 of those points. He totaled a record-setting 141 points for the entire tournament and was named the tournament's MVP (Most Valuable Player). Phog Allen's son Bob commented, "He absolutely won the NCAA by himself... He made 30 points or more every [tournament] game."

Now, Allen had another goal for his team: the Olympics. In 1936, Allen had helped get basketball introduced as an Olympic sport. In 1952, he was assistant coach of the USA's national team. Allen brought seven players from his 1952 squad to the Olympics. Led once again by Lovellette, the United States brought home a gold medal.

CHAPTER 2

NEW NAMES, NEW STYLES

In 1956, Doc Allen was seventy years old. According to Kansas University's rules, that meant he had to retire. Allen was not happy about being forced out, but he had no choice. The Kansas basketball team was turned over to his assistant, Dick Harp. It was difficult to take the place of someone as talented and loved as Allen, but Harp was a good man for the job. And he got a huge boost in his first season with a player named Wilt Chamberlain.

THE BIG DIPPER

Chamberlain came to Kansas in 1955 and immediately stood out. Back then, freshmen were not allowed to play on the varsity team. Instead, they had their own team. Coach Allen (who was in his last year) scheduled a game between the freshmen and the varsity squad. Chamberlain burst onto the court and scored a phenomenal 42 points. The freshmen won.

That kind of performance is rare, but Chamberlain was just getting started. The next season, he joined the varsity team. The first game was against Northwestern. Kansas won, 87–69, but it wasn't the score that people remembered afterward. It was the "Big Dipper"—a nickname Chamberlain had gotten because he had to dip his head to go through doorways. Chamberlain racked up unheard-of numbers during the game. He scored 52 points, setting a school record, which still stands. He also got thirty-one rebounds, which broke a school record at the time. He played all but half a minute of the entire game.

Posing with coach Dick Harp is the famous player Wilt Chamberlain, who dominated the Jayhawks during the two years he played varsity, before leaving to play professionally.

The Jayhawks went on to win twenty-one games in the 1956–1957 regular season, with only two losses. They went to the NCAA tournament, where Kansas breezed by Oklahoma City and San Francisco to reach the finals against North Carolina.

In that game, Kansas was behind at the half but battled back to tie the score and force the game into overtime. The first overtime period ended in another tie. So did the second overtime. The two teams, undoubtedly exhausted, now headed into a third overtime. With six seconds left, Kansas trailed by two. Kansas tried the only thing that might work: get the ball to super-scorer Wilt Chamberlain. Unfortunately for the Jayhawks, the pass to Chamberlain never reached him. A North Carolina player deflected it. The buzzer sounded, and Kansas lost. Even today, the game is considered one of the greatest ever played in NCAA history.

The 7'1" (2.1 m) Wilt Chamberlain had no trouble reaching the basket. He was known for his skill in dunking the ball, as he demonstrates during this 1957 practice at Allen Fieldhouse.

A TEAM WITHOUT WILT

In his first year at Kansas, Chamberlain scored 800 points, setting a school record that stood until Danny Manning broke it in 1987. He also totaled 510 rebounds, which still stands as a school record. During his time, Kansas compiled a 42–8 record. However, Chamberlain played varsity ball for only two years. He left after his junior year to join the professional team the Harlem Globetrotters. The Jayhawks suffered from losing such a great talent. In 1958–1959, Kansas won fewer than half its games.

However, the Jayhawks bounced back. Helped by players such as Bill Bridges, one of Kansas's great rebounders, the Jayhawks had high hopes for the 1960–1961 season. They'd had a couple of years to rebuild the team, and Kansas was a strong contender to go to the NCAA tournament in 1961.

CROSSING THE LINE

Wilt Chamberlain knew how to dunk the ball when he was near the basket, but his free throws were hit-or-miss—especially miss. So, Chamberlain came up with an unusual strategy. After taking a free throw, he would dive forward to catch his own shot, and then dunk it. Today, there's a rule against crossing the free throw line—and it's all because of Wilt.

There was a problem, though. The NCAA had been investigating Kansas. It concluded that the university had broken the rules in recruiting Wilt Chamberlain several years earlier. As punishment, Kansas could not participate in the tournament.

The next two years were tough on the Jayhawks. They posted losing records for both. That was the first time in almost sixty years that the team had two losing seasons in a row. The next year, the team just squeaked out a winning record at 13–12. It was clear Kansas was struggling. Coach Dick Harp decided to step down. Perhaps, with a new person in charge, the Jayhawks could improve.

THE WINNER WHO LOST

The new coach selected to lead the Jayhawks came from within the ranks. Ted Owens had worked as an assistant for Dick Harp. Owens worked to bring back the excitement that had faded in Harp's later years. He had murals painted showing some of Kansas's great moments from the past and put the names of legendary players on the lockers.

Allen Fieldhouse

In Allen Fieldhouse, Kansas's home arena, the seats aren't the most comfortable. But they're usually all filled anyway, if the Jayhawks are playing. The fieldhouse opened in 1955, after coach Phog Allen worked to get his players a better facility. Even though it's now almost fifty years old, many sportswriters still call it one of the best places in the country to watch a basketball game. Some of the best seats are reserved for the team's biggest fans: students. In 2010, the online magazine for ESPN named it the loudest arena in college basketball. Jayhawk fans proved that again in March 2012. They set a new level of loud, reaching 127 decibels—about as loud as a racecar engine or a chain saw.

After securing a berth in the Final Four, the Jayhawks win the semifinals in a close game against the Ohio State Buckeyes in 2010. Thomas Robinson celebrated with fans after the win.

Some great talent came to Kansas in the mid-1960s. Walt Wesley was a two-time all-American who averaged more than 19 points a game. Another two-time all-American was Joseph (JoJo) White. White led the Jayhawks to several victories before facing a bitter disappointment during the NCAA playoffs in 1966. At the end of the first overtime, the score was tied against Texas Western. White shot the ball, making the basket as the buzzer sounded. But the cheering from Kansas fans quickly died. An official ruled that White's foot had been out of bounds. The basket did not count. The game continued in another overtime, and Kansas eventually lost.

The Jayhawks had a few more strong years in the late 1960s and the early 1970s. The 1970–1971 team, led by Dave Robisch and Bud Stallworth, went to the Final Four—the four teams who play in the tournament semifinals. So did the 1973–1974 team. But Kansas lost both times. In 1981, the team got as far as the Sweet Sixteen, helped in part by Darnell Valentine, a strong player both on offense and defense. Valentine holds the school record for free throws and steals made during his career. However, in the 1982 and 1983 seasons, Kansas turned in losing records under Ted Owens.

In nineteen years, Owens had led the Jayhawks to more wins than any other coach except Allen. But good was not good enough. After two consecutive losing seasons, Owens was fired. Kansas wanted someone who would put the school back on the radar as a powerhouse program.

CHAPTER 3

MIRACLES CAN HAPPEN

Larry Brown seemed to bounce around more than a basketball. He was a great coach who turned losers into winners. But he had never stayed at a job for more than a few years. Sure, Larry Brown could come to Kansas. But would he stay? The university decided to take a chance. It hired Brown in 1983, and he stayed for five seasons. It wasn't long compared to other Kansas coaches, but it was long enough to bring Kansas another championship.

SHAKING THINGS UP

Brown had his own style. For one thing, he was superstitious. He never repeated anything he'd done before or during a loss—even if it had nothing to do with basketball. For example, one time he'd lost while wearing a paisley tie. He never wore another paisley tie. Another time, the Jayhawks lost after Brown had recorded a pregame radio show in the lobby. After that, he did them only inside arenas.

When Brown arrived at Kansas, he immediately started making changes. Not all of them were popular. He fired former Kansas player JoJo White, who had become an assistant coach under Owens. Instead,

Coach Larry Brown *(second from right)* speaks with star player Danny Manning *(center)* during a 1987 game. Brown led the team to a championship during his five-year stay at Kansas.

Brown wanted to hire Ed Manning, whom he had worked with before. Manning and his family—including his son, Danny—relocated to Lawrence. Soon after, the younger Manning, a 6-foot-10 (2.09 m) high school basketball star, announced that he planned to attend college at Kansas.

Brown's first season was rocky. The Jayhawk team had to adapt to a new coach and new ways of doing things. After each loss, Brown held team meetings. They analyzed what had gone wrong and how they might improve. Not everything was bad. Former coach Owens had spent his last years at Kansas working hard to recruit good players. There definitely was talent in the 1983–1984 squad that Brown inherited. Brown was skeptical at first, saying, "When I saw the films of

GAINING SELF-CONFIDENCE

In the 1980s, when Larry Brown was running a basketball camp in Kansas, a player from Oklahoma State University hurt his knee. Brown felt terrible and offered to help the player in any way he could. The young man responded by telling Brown he could give him a job after he graduated. Brown agreed but then seemed to forget about the incident. The OSU graduate did not. A few months later, he showed up in Brown's office, ready to work. It turned into the first coaching job of many for Bill Self, who is now the Jayhawks' head coach.

last year, I was not that encouraged... but after being around the kids more, seeing how they've grown up, I get more encouraged each day." He molded the team's style of play to best fit his players' abilities. Slowly, the Jayhawk team started to come together. By the end of the season, Kansas had earned a trip to the NCAA tournament. They were knocked out in the second round, but the Jayhawks were ready for the next year.

STEPPING UP

As Larry Brown entered his second season at Kansas, he got a new freshman recruit: Ed Manning's son, Danny. Teammates remember Danny as being quiet and somewhat shy. Brown already had a good team. As a new, young player, Danny didn't want to overstep his bounds. But the other Jayhawks soon recognized his potential. He could be a huge asset to the team. He just had to step up and do it. Teammate Mark Turgeon remembers telling Manning once, "Danny, you've got

Danny Manning resists the defense of a Duke guard during a 1987 NCAA semifinal game, scoring 25 points in the Jayhawks' 66–59 win, and propelling the team to the finals.

to shoot. For us to win, you have to shoot."

The team was starting to gel, but the payoff was still out of reach. Tough losses stung the Jayhawks in 1984–1985. Again, they were eliminated from the NCAA playoffs in the second round. Frustrated by the results, Brown clamped down on his players. He wanted his team to play hard—but only if they were playing basketball. Over the summer, he set a nightly curfew, expecting his players to focus on two things: school and basketball. Meanwhile, Brown also worked to get fans fired up about the team. In 1985, he held the first "Late Night in the Phog." This huge pep rally is now a tradition. It happens at midnight in Allen Fieldhouse to celebrate the opening of each season.

Brown's strategy worked. The Jayhawks steamrolled through their schedule in 1985–1986, finishing the season with a 31–3 record. The momentum carried into the NCAA tournament. Kansas racked up another four wins. The team headed into the Final Four for a matchup against Duke. Their luck ended there with a 71–67 loss. Danny Manning, Kansas's dependable scorer, had managed only four points for the entire game. Worse, another player, Archie Marshall, hurt his knee during the game. The injury kept him from playing the next season. The 1986–1987 season ended with a 25–11 record and another trip to the NCAA tournament. This time, Kansas advanced to the "Sweet Sixteen" but was beaten by Georgetown.

Meanwhile, people were starting to talk. Larry Brown had been with Kansas four years but had not gotten the big win at the NCAA tournament. Would he stick around? Just as important, what was going through Danny Manning's head? He'd completed his junior year and was a star. College basketball doesn't pay, but professional does. Would he take the money and go pro?

DANNY AND THE MIRACLES

Both Brown and Manning decided to stick with Kansas for the 1987–1988 season. The year got off to a slow start. The team had strong players in Kevin Pritchard and Milt Newton, but many of the team's other members were unable to play. Chris Piper was recovering from surgery. Archie Marshall had healed from his knee injury but only got to play a few games before he hurt it again. This time, he was out for good. Marvin Branch, the team's starting center, could not play the second half of the season because his grades were not good enough. The Jayhawks were still winning more games than they were losing, but not by much.

Then things turned around. Brown called in different players, and win followed win until the Jayhawks found themselves in the NCAA tournament. That was something few people expected after the season's rocky start, but it was just the beginning. Kansas moved on to the finals. Their opponent was Oklahoma. Kansas was clearly the underdog.

Kansas's Kevin Pritchard *(left)* concentrates on defending Andre Boyd of Robert Morris during this 1990 NCAA early playoff game. Kansas won and advanced to the next round.

The powerhouse Sooners had been averaging more than 100 per game. Kansas had already lost twice to them earlier in the year.

But Kansas kept pace with Oklahoma. Senior Danny Manning scored an incredible 31 points, including four free throws in the final minute. That was enough for Kansas to stun the Sooners with a final score of 83–79. For his efforts, Manning was awarded the game's MVP award. He also became Kansas's all-time leading scorer, ending his career with 2,951 points. It was Danny's show all night, and to many Jayhawk fans, the win was indeed a miracle.

CHAPTER 4

KNOCKING AT THE DOOR

People had wondered whether Larry Brown would leave Kansas before the 1987–1988 season. They wondered the same thing after it ended. Four days after winning the national championship, rumors spread that Brown was going to coach at UCLA. Brown announced he would stay at Kansas, but then he changed his mind. Two months later, he quit and took a job with the San Antonio Spurs.

ROY WILLIAMS

Kansas was left scrambling for a new coach. Bob Frederick, Kansas's athletics director, called the head coach at the University of North Carolina, Dean Smith. Smith had played for the Kansas basketball team in the 1950s and had briefly worked as an assistant coach to the team. Smith did not want the job, but he made a suggestion. He thought one of his assistant coaches, Roy Williams, would be a good choice. Williams did not have any head coaching experience. Frederick decided that was OK. He was more interested in someone who would become part of the Kansas "family."

Williams inherited a lot of problems. Once again, the NCAA was investigating Kansas's recruiting practices.

Once again, Kansas had broken some rules. As a penalty, the team was barred from participating in any postseason games the next year. Kansas would not be allowed to defend its title. In addition, there were limits on what the university could do to recruit new players in the next few years. Williams was disappointed that Kansas would not be eligible to play in the tournament. But the recruitment restrictions worried him even more. Almost immediately, potential players canceled their visits to Kansas. Nonetheless, Williams tried to remain positive.

Coach Roy Williams speaks to his team during practices for NCAA regional playoffs in 1994. Williams did not win a national championship for the Jayhawks, but was one of the team's most-loved coaches.

The Jayhawks started strong in the 1988–1989 season but then lost eight in a row as they battled stronger teams and suffered injuries. In one close game, the Jayhawks managed to drag the number-one-ranked Oklahoma into overtime. Kansas ended up losing, but Williams was proud of his team's effort. Afterward, the crowd gave them a standing ovation.

The North Carolina Connection

Over the years, the basketball programs at Kansas and North Carolina have been intertwined. Several people have coached for both schools. Kansas fans rooted for the Tar Heels in their games, and vice versa. The teams rarely faced each other, though, except in tournaments. UNC coach Dean Smith once asked, "Why play against someone you consider a friend?" After Roy Williams left Kansas and returned to coach at North Carolina, the two schools became fiercer rivals.

MAKING A COMEBACK

Kansas ended the 1989 season with a mediocre record. No one seemed to expect much from the next year's team. The coaches and sportswriters who ranked the teams skipped over Kansas. One magazine even predicted that Kansas would come in dead last in the conference.

Then Kansas breezed by Alabama-Birmingham in a preseason game. Next it beat Louisiana State. Then Las Vegas. Then St. John's. Now people started to take notice. In the next poll, Kansas leaped into second place.

The Jayhawks won nineteen games in a row, climbing to the number-one spot, before falling to Missouri. But they bounced back to beat Kansas State and win the next four games. The season ended with two more losses, including a second loss to Missouri and another to Oklahoma. Still, the Jayhawks had posted a phenomenal season that no one had expected.

Before coming to Kansas, Roy Williams *(right, standing)* worked at the University of North Carolina with head coach Dean Smith *(left, standing)*, who played basketball for KU under Doc Allen.

Kansas entered the 1990–1991 season ranked much higher. Williams wasn't sure the experts had it right. He didn't think his team was as strong as the year before. The Jayhawks lost their first two conference games, to Oklahoma and Oklahoma State. Still, Williams was determined to lead his team as far as possible. As the season went on, the Jayhawk team started playing better and reached the Final Four.

They were slated to play North Carolina in the semifinals. Williams would face his mentor, Dean Smith. Williams didn't exactly like the idea of competing with Smith, or of playing against the school that had been his home for many years. On the other hand, he sure didn't want to lose.

And he didn't. Kansas pulled out a 79–73 win to advance to the finals. There, however, they lost to Duke. It would

Wilt Returns

Forty years after he left, one of Kansas's star players returned. In 1998, Wilt Chamberlain came to see his jersey, number 13, retired and hung up in Allen Fieldhouse. In a speech, he remembered the loss to North Carolina in 1957, saying he felt he had disappointed his teammates. Over the years, Chamberlain had sometimes indicated that he did not enjoy his time at Kansas. Now he seemed to have mellowed. "I've learned in life that you have to take the bitter with the sweet, and how sweet this is," he said. "I'm a Jayhawk and I'm proud to be a part of the tradition here." Chamberlain died the next year from heart trouble.

take eleven more years for Williams to take the Jayhawks to an NCAA final.

A Decade of Disappointment

The 1990s brought some successes. The team brought home conference tournament championships. They regularly played in the NCAA playoffs and reached the Final Four in 1992. Several great players passed through the Kansas ranks. Jacque Vaughn and Paul Pierce played for the 1996–1997 team, often considered one of Kansas's greatest.

In 2002, power players Kirk Hinrich, Nick Collison, and Drew Gooden helped take Kansas to the Final Four again. The Jayhawks lost to Maryland, but Williams got another shot at the championship in 2003. Gooden was gone, but the Jayhawks still reached the finals against Syracuse with the help of Hinrich, Collison, and Keith Langford.

Kirk Hinrich keeps his eye on the prize as he pushes past a Kansas State defender in this 2002 game. The final score of 103–68 delivered a decisive win to the Jayhawks.

Unfortunately, the disappointments that had come to the Jayhawks for so many years were not over. "Syracuse came out and hit us right in the mouth," Williams said later. At one point, Kansas was down by 18. The Jayhawks clawed their way back up, but in the end the Orangemen pulled out a 3-point win, 81–78.

Immediately after the game, rumors started that Williams would return to North Carolina. A week later, he confirmed he was leaving. After fifteen years with the beloved Williams in charge, Jayhawk fans were shocked and devastated.

"We've been knocking on the door [to win a national title]," Roy Williams had said once, "and we're going to keep knocking until we knock it down."

Eventually, the Jayhawks would knock it down—but they would do it without Roy.

Chapter 5

BACK ON TOP

Bill Self's chair was ready for him. He was at the press conference announcing him as the Jayhawks' next coach. He walked up to his seat, put his hands on it, and said, "Feels hot." Everyone laughed as Self showed his easy sense of humor. Taking over for Roy Williams would indeed put Self in the "hot seat." There had been agonizing losses under Williams, and then the loss of Williams himself. Everyone was watching to see how Self would perform.

REBUILDING A TEAM

Self inherited a team that had been put together by Roy Williams. There were some adjustments that had to be made, but Self did well. In his first year, 2003–2004, he led Kansas to a 24–9 record. The team made it to the Elite Eight in the NCAA tournament. The next two years weren't quite as successful for the Jayhawks. Self remembered, "We couldn't get out of our own way." The Jayhawks rebounded in 2006–2007, beating the Texas Longhorns to win the Big 12 conference championship. Next, the Jayhawks went to the NCAA tournament, again making it as far as the Elite Eight before losing to UCLA.

Head coach Bill Self speaks to players during a timeout in a game against Chattanooga in 2012. The Jayhawks reached the NCAA finals earlier that year, but lost to Kentucky.

In the 2007–2008 season, it seemed Kansas was unstoppable. They went twenty games without a loss. The game that did finally end the streak was a strange one. Kansas has had an in-state rivalry with the Kansas State Wildcats for decades. However, the Jayhawks are the dominant team. When they took to the road to meet the Wildcats, they'd lost only once to Kansas State since 1994. In the end, however, the Wildcats walked away with an 84–75 victory. The Jayhawks lost two more times in the early months of 2008. One was a 3-point loss to Texas. The other was a 1-point squeaker to Oklahoma State. But by the time March Madness rolled around, it didn't matter.

During the last ten days of March, Kansas plowed through the NCAA tournament. With Sherron Collins, Mario Chalmers, Brandon Rush, Russell Robinson, and others, Kansas easily polished off its opponents. The only close game was against Davidson, which Kansas eventually won 59–57. Every few days, the number of teams still in the running got cut in half. Sixty-four went to thirty-two. Then it was the Sweet Sixteen. The Elite Eight. Kansas was still alive. Then came the Final Four. In this game, Kansas would face its greatest challenge yet: North Carolina.

Former Kansas coach Roy Williams was leading the Tar Heels. It was an emotional moment. It wasn't only the NCAA tournament at stake. Thousands of Jayhawk fans felt their pride was on the line. Perhaps the players felt the same way because Kansas went on a 40–12 scoring run against North Carolina early in the game. That paved the way for their eventual 84–66 win. The Jayhawks were in the finals. Next up, Memphis.

MARIO'S MIRACLE

Memphis had lost only one game all season when Kansas faced them in the finals. During the first half, the teams played a close game, ending with a 5-point lead for Kansas. Memphis fought back in the second half, however. At one point they were ahead by 9 points. Kansas narrowed the gap again but didn't quite close it. With a minute left, the Jayhawks were still down by 2. Then, with only ten seconds left, Memphis player Derrick Rose sank a free throw. Now the Jayhawks were behind by 3. The clock ticked down. The

After "The Shot": Mario Chalmers celebrates after his 3-point field goal tied the game against Memphis in the 2008 NCAA final and pushed the game into overtime. Kansas went on to win the championship.

only thing that could save the Jayhawks was a 3-pointer, a near-miracle with only two seconds left.

And then they got it. Taking a pass from Sherron Collins, Mario Chalmers stood on the 3-point line, took aim, and shot. The ball swished in, nothing but net. The scoreboard ticked up three more on the Jayhawk side, tying the game, and the buzzer sounded. "Mario's Miracle" had sent the game into overtime. The Jayhawks still had to win it, but the excitement and momentum carried them through. They came out 75–68 winners.

"As soon as it left my hand it felt good, and I knew it was going in," Chalmers revealed afterward. "I could've turned around and thrown the ball between my legs and it would've gone in. That's how confident I was."

MARIO'S MIRACLE, TAKE TWO

In 2011, the NBA was squabbling. All games were canceled until they could work out their differences. Kansas decided to take advantage of the situation. The university decided to hold a game for former Jayhawk players. The game, called "Legends of the Phog," included many NBA players who would not normally have been able to come. Late in the game, the score was tied at 108. Then Paul Pierce made a 3-pointer to pull his team ahead. With only a few seconds left, the ball went to the other team, into the hands of Mario Chalmers. Now his team needed a 3-pointer to tie. Spectators remembered the time three years earlier, when Chalmers had made the shot against Memphis. Could he do it again? He could. The shot went in, but this time, there was no overtime. The game ended in a tie.

KEEPING THE MOMENTUM

Kansas ended the 2008 season with thirty-seven wins, the best in the school's history. The talent on the Jayhawk team became even more obvious when five players were chosen in the NBA draft. There was a downside to that, though. When the team returned for the 2008–2009 season, six top scorers were gone. Still, the Jayhawks won the conference championship and made it to the Sweet Sixteen of the NCAA

Senior guard Elijah Johnson celebrates the Jayhawks' 59–55 win over their in-state rival, the Kansas State Wildcats, in this 2013 game played in Manhattan, Kansas.

tournament. The next few years, Kansas played solidly. In 2011, the team advanced to the Elite Eight before being eliminated.

Things didn't look as promising for the 2011–2012 team. Only one starter returned, and seven regular players from the previous year were gone. At one point, Bill Self met with former coach Larry Brown to look over the Jayhawk team. They wondered if the team could even make it to the tournament at all.

Their doubt was soon erased. Kansas finished the regular season at 26–5. They advanced through the NCAA tournament all the way to the finals. There, they played Kentucky, the number-one-ranked team in the country. Kentucky was loaded with players who would be drafted by the NBA just a few months later. Kansas made a good effort in the game, but in the end they were just outplayed. They lost, 67–59.

Nonetheless, by the end of the 2012 season, Kansas had posted some impressive statistics. The Jayhawks had won a remarkable 87 percent of their games over the last six seasons. That made them the winningest team in Divison I basketball.

At Kansas, though, it doesn't come down to wins and losses. Sure, the wins are celebrated, and some of the losses hurt. But what matters to most Kansas basketball players is simply the chance to wear the crimson and blue, to run out on the court as fans shout "Rock, Chalk, Jayhawk," and to be a part of the long Kansas tradition.

Timeline

1891: James Naismith invents the game of basketball.

1898: Naismith forms a basketball team at the University of Kansas; the men lose their first game.

1919: Forrest "Phog" Allen takes over as coach of the Jayhawks.

1922: Kansas wins the Helms Foundation national championship.

1923: The Jayhawks win their second consecutive national championship.

1939: Allen helps establish the NCAA tournament.

1940: Kansas has its first trip to the NCAA finals but loses to Indiana.

1952: Led by Clyde Lovellette, the Jayhawks win their first NCAA championship with a victory over St. John's.

1955: Legendary player Wilt Chamberlain comes to Kansas; Allen Fieldhouse opens.

1956: Phog Allen retires.

1957: Kansas loses the NCAA championship in a triple-overtime loss to North Carolina.

1966: Kansas suffers an overtime loss to Texas Western in the final game of the NCAA tournament.

1983: Larry Brown hired as head coach.

1984: Danny Manning comes to Kansas University.

1985: "Late Night in the Phog" tradition begins under Larry Brown.

1988: "Danny and the Miracles" lead KU to its second NCAA championship; Roy Williams hired as head coach.

1991: The Jayhawks beat North Carolina to advance to the NCAA finals but lose to Duke.

1998: Kansas basketball celebrates its 100th anniversary.

2003: Kansas loses to Syracuse in the NCAA championship; Bill Self becomes the head coach of the Jayhawks.

2008: Kansas defeats Memphis to win its third NCAA championship; the Jayhawks set a school record for most wins in a single season.

2012: Kansas falls to Kentucky in the NCAA championship.

GLOSSARY

agonizing Extremely painful; causing hurt.

all-American A player chosen as one of the best in the nation.

consecutive Coming right in a row, one after the other.

contender A participant who has a good chance in a particular competitive environment.

decibel A scientific way of measuring the loudness of sound.

deficit Having less of something than is needed.

deflect To redirect something; to prevent something from reaching its target.

draft The event during which professional sports teams choose college players to join the team.

gel To come together; to begin to work successfully.

legacy The long-term influence and contributions that a person or group of people leaves.

March Madness The period in March when the NCAA basketball tournament is held.

paisley A specific type of pattern printed on fabric and other material.

potential A promising but not proven ability to do something.

prestigious Respected; important.

rally To recover; to come back from a weak position.

skeptical Doubtful; hesitant to believe in something.

FOR MORE INFORMATION

Big 12 Conference

400 East John Carpenter Freeway

Irving, TX 75062

(469) 524-1000

Web site: http://www.big12sports.com

The Big 12 Conference is comprised of ten colleges, including the University of Kansas. The organization oversees play within the conference and organizes competitions.

The College Basketball Experience

1401Grand Boulevard

Kansas City, MO 64106

(816) 949-7500

Web site: http://www.collegebasketballexperience.com

A hands-on history of men's college basketball is on display at the National Collegiate Basketball Hall of Fame, part of the College Basketball Experience.

Kansas Athletics

Allen Fieldhouse

1651 Naismith Drive

Lawrence, KS 66045

(785) 864-8200

Web site: http://www.kuathletics.com

The athletics department for the University of Kansas manages the college's sports teams and maintains a comprehensive Web site with information about players and games.

Naismith Memorial Basketball Hall of Fame

1000 Hall of Fame Avenue
Springfield, MA 01105
(877) 446-6752
Web site: http://www.hoophall.com

Almost three hundred inductees and a host of basketball history come together at the Naismith Memorial Basketball Hall of Fame, located in the town where the game was invented.

National Association of Basketball Coaches (NABC)

1111 Main Street, Suite 1000
Kansas City, MO 64105-2136
(816) 878-6222
Web site: http://www.nabc.org

The NABC works to promote the interests of basketball coaches and players by supporting the principles of sportsmanship and integrity, as well as to work with the NCAA on policies.

National Basketball Association (NBA)

645 Fifth Avenue
New York, NY 10022
(212) 407-8000
Web site: http://www.nba.com

The NBA represents professional basketball teams in the United States. Its aim is to promote and regulate the sport.

National Collegiate Athletic Association (NCAA)

700 W. Washington Street
P.O. Box 6222
Indianapolis, IN 46206-6222

(317) 917-6222

Web site: http://www.ncaa.org

The NCAA represents student athletes in all college sports and across all levels of play. Each of its three divisions creates and enforces regulations and organizes competitive play among its members.

U.S. Basketball Writers Association (USBWA)

1818 Chouteau Avenue

St. Louis, MO 63103

E-mail: webmaster@sportswriters.net

Web site: http://www.sportswriters.net/usbwa

Founded in 1956, the USBWA is comprised of media professionals who write about the sport of basketball. Members participate in selecting a "Player of the Year" and "Coach of the Year."

WEB SITES

Due to the changing nature of Internet links, Rosen Publishing has developed an online list of Web sites related to the subject of this book. This site is updated regularly. Please use this link to access the list:

http://www.rosenlinks.com/AMWT/KSBB

FOR FURTHER READING

Berman, Len. *The Greatest Moments in Sports: Upsets and Underdogs.* Naperville, IL: Sourcebooks Jabberwocky, 2012.

Bohnert, Suzy Beamer. *Game-Day Youth: Learning Basketball's Lingo.* Arlington, VA: B&B Publishing, 2011.

Christopher, Matt. *Great Moments in Basketball History*. New York, NY: Little, Brown Books for Young Readers, 2009.

Doeden, Matt. *Wilt Chamberlain*. Minneapolis, MN: Twenty-First Century Books, 2010.

Gigliotti, Jim. *College Basketball Guide: All the Teams, All the Stars, All the Big Games.* Santa Barbara, CA: Beach Ball Books, 2010.

LeBoutillier, Nate. *Play Basketball Like a Pro: Key Skills and Tips.* Mankato, MN: Capstone Press, 2010.

Monnig, Alex. *North Carolina Tar Heels.* Minneapolis, MN: ABDO Publishing, 2012.

Schulte, Mary. *The Final Four: All About College Basketball's Biggest Event*. Mankato, MN: Capstone Press, 2012.

Silverman, Drew. *Kansas Jayhawks.* Minneapolis, MN: ABDO Publishing, 2012.

Slade, Suzanne. *Basketball: How It Works.* Mankato, MN: Capstone Press, 2010.

Sommers, Michael. *Basketball in the Big 12 Conference.* New York, NY: Rosen Publishing, 2008.

Stewart, Mark, and Mike Kennedy. *Swish: The Quest for Basketball's Perfect Shot*. Minneapolis, MN: Millbrook Press, 2009.

BIBLIOGRAPHY

Buckner, Steve. *Game of My Life: Memorable Stories of Kansas Jayhawks Basketball.* Champaign, IL: Sports Publishing, LLC, 2007.

Garrity, John. "He's Manning for the Future." SportsIllustrated.CNN.com, October 17, 1983. Retrieved July 16, 2012 (http://sportsillustrated.cnn.com/vault/article/magazine/MAG1121385/index.htm).

Hendel, John. *Kansas Jayhawks: History-Making Basketball.* Lenexa, KS: Quality Sports Publications, 1991.

Jenks, Jayson. "The Rules of the Game." Grantland.com, March 16, 2012. Retrieved July 14, 2012 (http://www.grantland.com/story/_/id/7692635/dr-james-naismith-bill-self-history-basketball-kansas).

Kansas University Alumni Association. *The Champions: Kansas Basketball at the Pinnacle.* Denver, CO: Rich Clarkson and Associates, 2008.

Kerkhoff, Blair. *A Century of Jayhawk Triumphs: The 100 Greatest Victories in the History of Kansas Basketball.* Lenexa, KS: Addax Publishing Group, 1997.

King, Jason. *Beyond the Phog: Untold Stories from Kansas Basketball's Most Dominant Decade.* Taunton, MA: Quebecor World, 2011.

Nelson, Eric, and Lauretta McMillen. *Crimson and Blue Handbook: Stories, Stats, and Stuff About KU Basketball.* Wichita, KS: The Wichita Eagle and Beacon Publishing Co., 1996.

Self, Bill, and John Rohde. *Bill Self: At Home in the Phog.* Overland Park, KS: Ascend Media, LLC, 2008.

Smith, Gary. "'Where You Gonna Be Next Year, Larry?'" Sports Illustrated.CNN.com, November 12, 1984. Retrieved July 16, 2012 (http://sportsillustrated.cnn.com/vault/article/magazine/MAG1122831/1/index.htm).

Sports Illustrated, NCAA Men's Basketball Champion, Kansas Commemorative, 2008 Issue. New York, NY: Time Inc. Magazine Company, 2008.

Stallard, Mark. *Tales from the Kansas Jayhawks Locker Room: A Collection of the Greatest Jayhawks Basketball Stories Ever Told.* New York, NY: Sports Publishing, 2012.

Woodling, Chuck, John McLendon, and Alexander Wolff. *The Kansas Century: 100 Years of Championship Jayhawk Basketball.* Kansas City, MO: Andrews McMeel Publishing, 1997.

INDEX

ABOUT THE AUTHOR

Diane Bailey has written about twenty-five nonfiction books for teens, on subjects ranging from sports to states to celebrities. Her first novel, *Murder a Cappella*, a murder mystery, was published in 2012. Diane also works as an editor for other children's authors. She has two sons and two dogs, and lives in Kansas.

PHOTO CREDITS

Cover, pp. 1, 5, 16, 32 Jamie Squire/Getty Images; back cover (hoop) Mike Flippo/ Shutterstock.com; p. 4 Erick W. Rasco/ Sports Illustrated/Getty Images; pp. 6, 12, 18, 24, 31 Todd Warshaw/Getty Images; pp. 7, 9, 11, 13, 14, 21, 23, 25, 29, 34 © AP Images; p. 19 David E. Klutho/Sports Illustrated/ Getty Images; p. 27 James Drake/Sports Illustrated/Getty Images; p. 36 Kansas City Star/McClatchy-Tribune/Getty Images; multiple interior page borders and boxed text backgrounds (basketball) Mark Cinotti/ Shutterstock.com; back cover and multiple interior pages background (abstract pattern) © iStockphoto.com/Che McPherson.

Designer: Brian Garvey; Editor: Bethany Bryan
Photo Researcher: Marty Levick